Published in 2022 by Groundwood Books / House of Anansi Press
groundwoodbooks.com

Groundwood Books respectfully acknowledges that the land on which we operate is the Traditional Territory of many Nations, including the Anishinabeg, the Wendat and the Haudenosaunee. It is also the Treaty Lands of the Mississaugas of the Credit.

We gratefully acknowledge for their financial support of our publishing program the Canada Council for the Arts, the Ontario Arts Council and the Government of Canada.

Canada Council   Conseil des Arts
for the Arts   du Canada

ONTARIO ARTS COUNCIL
CONSEIL DES ARTS DE L'ONTARIO
an Ontario government agency
un organisme du gouvernement de l'Ontario

With the participation of the Government of Canada
Avec la participation du gouvernement du Canada | Canadä

Library and Archives Canada Cataloguing in Publication
Title: City streets are for people / written by Andrea Curtis ; illustrated by Emma FitzGerald.
Names: Curtis, Andrea, author. | FitzGerald, Emma, illustrator.
Description: Series statement: ThinkCities
Identifiers: Canadiana (print) 20210230533 | Canadiana (ebook) 20210250585 | ISBN 9781773064659 (hardcover) | ISBN 9781773064666 (EPUB) | ISBN 9781773064673 (Kindle)
Subjects: LCSH: Urban transportation—Environmental aspects—Juvenile literature. | LCSH: Sustainable transportation—Juvenile literature.
Classification: LCC HE305 .C87 2022 | DDC j388.4—dc23

The illustrations were sketched by hand with black pen on paper and colored digitally in Photoshop, with additional layers of color added using pencil crayon and watercolor.
Design by Michael Solomon
Printed and bound in China

MIX
Paper from
responsible sources
FSC® C144853
www.fsc.org

For Nick, who helped me imagine
what living in the city could be
— AC

To all those many minds and hearts
dedicated to making our cities more
livable and equitable — EF

CITY STREETS ARE FOR PEOPLE

WRITTEN BY
ANDREA CURTIS

ILLUSTRATED BY
EMMA FITZGERALD

Groundwood Books
House of Anansi Press
Toronto / Berkeley

CITY STREETS can be noisy and crowded, dirty and sometimes even scary. In many cities, cars and trucks rule the roads. Sidewalks are narrow or don't exist at all. Kids on foot or riding bicycles and scooters have to dodge and weave, competing with fast-moving metal machines. Buses, streetcars and trains can be so jammed it's hard to move.

Transportation is connected to everything we do — from visiting Grandma's house or the library to moving goods and people down the street and around the globe. In fact, figuring out how to get around with the least possible impact on the planet has turned into one of the biggest challenges of our time.

That's because transportation is a huge contributor to our climate crisis. More than 90 percent of vehicles run on oil and gas (known as fossil fuels), which, when burned, release carbon dioxide and contribute to global warming.

Cars and trucks also spew other types of pollution into the air. This can lead to serious health issues like cancer and heart disease, as well as breathing problems like asthma.

Plus, boxing ourselves up inside cars makes us inactive and disconnected from one another. Traffic accidents are also the leading cause of death for kids and young adults.

But it doesn't have to be this way.

All over the world, people are reimagining transit and their cities. We're taking over sidewalks to talk and dance, to eat and play. We're making room for bike lanes and electric scooters. We're building green transportation and reclaiming public spaces.

City streets are for people!

The oldest cities weren't built for cars and trucks. Some of the narrow, twisty streets in Paris, France, or Jerusalem, Israel, aren't even wide enough for three people to walk side by side.

The largest vehicles in these early cities were wagons pulled by a horse, cow or mule. Even today, you can find spots where horses were once tied up in Florence, Italy, or Brooklyn, New York.

The omnibus, the first regular public transportation, appeared in the 1820s in France and England. These horse-drawn carriages carried up to fifty passengers at a time. There were no fixed stops — people simply signaled when they wanted to get on or off.

Streetcars running on metal rail lines and pulled by horses were the next innovation. These "horsecars" carried more people and offered a less bumpy ride. The streetcar system in Toronto, Ontario, used horsepower until 1892!

In the 1890s, bicycle fever hit cities worldwide. More affordable, faster and easier to ride than older models, the new bikes reshaped the streets as cyclists pushed for smoother paved roads.

Powered by steam engines, trains changed transportation in the early 1800s. They made it possible to move people and cargo farther and faster on rail lines that eventually criss-crossed continents.

The first subway also ran on steam power. It opened in London, England, in 1863. A locomotive pulled carriages lit by gas lamps, and smoke and soot often filled the passageways. It took another thirty years before the Tube (named for its cylinder-shaped tunnels) moved to electricity.

In the early 1900s, automobiles started to be mass-produced, and cities changed again. Most places weren't built for so many fast-moving vehicles, and streets became busier, louder and more dangerous.

In North America, especially, cars took over. Streets were widened, and lots of space was devoted to parking. Cities sprawled outward, and suburbs and a web of roads and highways were built. At the same time, investment in public transportation dropped off, and the systems started to break down.

Today we are at a crossroads. As more and more people move into urban centers, and the climate emergency deepens, people everywhere are calling for a big rethink about how we get around.

We want greener, safer, better-organized transit to serve our growing numbers. We want cities where everyone has a chance to thrive.

That's why Madrid, Spain, bans older gas and diesel-powered cars from the city center. In Copenhagen,

Denmark, it's so easy and safe to cycle, there are more bikes than people! And the nation of Luxembourg has made all public transit free, because it will help the environment and make life affordable for everyone.

Cities all over the world are encouraging drivers to give up their old, polluting vehicles. They're turning parking spaces into bike lanes and demanding speed limits around schools. They're building housing and businesses near public transit so we don't need to drive.

It turns out we're happier and healthier when we spend less time in cars and more time meeting neighbors, exploring with friends and enjoying the bustling city around us.

13

Public transit is how most people get around large urban centers. In London, England, and Manhattan, New York, more than half the residents don't even own cars.

Shared transportation saves energy because one vehicle moves many people. A single subway car can hold about one hundred riders at a time — and helps limit the number of cars jamming busy streets.

But in order to be sustainable (so we don't destroy or completely use up the earth's resources), mass transit must be powered by clean, renewable energy — such as electricity generated by water, sun or wind.

People choose to take transit when it's reliable, affordable and safe. It also needs to be convenient, with interconnected bus, train, streetcar, bikeshare and subway systems, so it's easy to hop from one to another.

Many of us care deeply about public transportation because we use it every day. At its best, transit is a moving public space. It belongs to all of us.

In many cities, buses are the most common mode
of transit. We might jump on a mini, a double-decker
or maybe an extra-long bus with an accordion-like
midsection that twists around corners.

Buses are a cheap and effective way to move
people, whether it's to school, dance
class or to pick up groceries. One bus
can replace at least thirty cars on
the road! Routes can be switched
or added as demand changes,
and they often reach low-income
communities that don't have other
transit options.

Researchers also say it's safer
to travel in a bus than a car. Many
cities are testing self-driving buses
— with no human at the wheel —
and some say they're safer still.

Though most buses are powered by gas or diesel, in Adelaide, Australia, electric buses are charged by solar panels on the station roof. There are buses in Bristol, England, that are fueled with gas made from food waste!

Bogotá, the capital of Colombia, is known around the globe for its well-organized rapid bus system, where buses drive in dedicated lanes, skipping the heavy traffic. Since the system was introduced, road-related deaths and air pollution have both gone down.

Painted fire-engine red or electric yellow, streetcars (sometimes called trams or trolleys) make cities like New Orleans, Louisiana, and Lisbon, Portugal, look like the set for an old movie.

Streetcars have seen a revival recently, and cities such as Strasbourg, France, have reconstructed old tramways with quieter, energy-efficient vehicles. In Hong Kong, China, the trams are all double-deckers.

Many streetcar tracks share the road with cars and buses, and though trams were once powered by steam, they now mostly run on electricity fed by overhead wires. Wuppertal, Germany, is home to an electric train more than a century old, which hangs from a track suspended 40 feet (12 m) over the city!

Electric-powered light rail transit (LRT) systems are similar to streetcar lines, but the trains are quicker, stop less often and can carry more people. Many LRT networks have their own lanes, separate from road traffic. Cities are investing in LRT because it's less expensive and faster to build than subways.

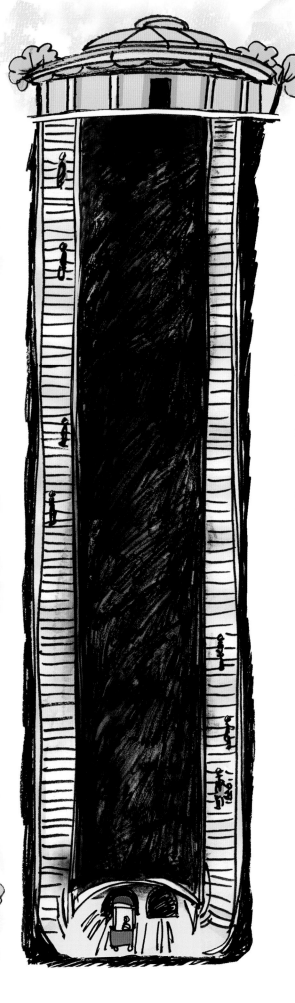

Zooming below the streets, emerging into open air, even running beneath rivers, subways carry lots of people, reduce pollution and help keep traffic off the roads. They're also the speediest mode of city transit.

With 400-plus stations extending over hundreds of miles, the subway in Beijing, China, averages more than ten million riders per day. On such busy subway systems, workers are hired during peak times to push people inside before the doors close!

But subways are expensive to build and maintain because they must be far underground. One of the deepest stations in the world is in Moscow, Russia, reaching down inside the earth as far as a nineteen-storey building.

Moscow is also known for the beauty of its stations, with chandeliers twinkling from soaring ceilings. In Seoul, South Korea, many of the subway trains are outfitted with air-conditioning, heated seats and free Wi-Fi.

Commuter trains carrying kids and their families from suburbs or neighboring towns into the city are a key piece of the urban transportation puzzle.

When these trains are affordable, comfortable and on time, people choose them instead of driving downtown. And it's better still if they're fueled by renewable sources, like the Dutch trains that run on 100 percent wind power.

Trains are also one of the most environmentally friendly forms of long-distance travel, since most high-speed trains are powered by electricity. Racing along tracks at up

to 155 miles (250 km) an hour, they shrink the distance between major cities in Europe and Asia. In Spain, bullet trains travel from Madrid to Barcelona in less than three hours — three times faster than an old-style railcar.

The Shanghai Maglev train uses environmentally friendly technology known as magnetic levitation that allows it to float above the track. Sleek and streamlined, it travels at more than twice the speed of bullet trains. China and Japan are working on new maglev trains that reach speeds of 373 miles (600 km) an hour!

Imagine gliding to school or to visit a pal on public transportation that floats. That's what kids do in Stockholm, Sweden, where ferries are part of the transit system.

Some cities built on water, such as Venice, Italy, and Amsterdam in the Netherlands, have never given up their marine connections. Others are returning to floating transit for relief from crushing traffic jams. The ferries in Lagos, Nigeria, allow kids and their parents to get from one end of the city to the other in thirty minutes, compared to half a day in a car!

High safety standards for water travel mean ferries can be expensive to operate. And most passenger boats use fossil fuels. But as technology improves and citizens push for greener options, cities such as Toronto, Ontario, and Fredrikstad, Norway, are introducing electric boats to their fleets.

What do you do when your soccer game is at the bottom of a mountain and you live at the top? Take a high-flying cable car, of course!

Many of us think of these aerial lifts as something you see at a ski hill or tourist attraction. But in Medellín, Colombia, and La Paz, Bolivia, they're used for daily commuting. The electric-powered transit system floats above the crowded roads and connects people living in remote and often poor hillside areas to the rest of the city.

Other cities have also built public transportation to suit their geography. Naples, Italy, has funiculars — trams that move up and down the hills on a track attached to a cable. Hong Kong, China, helps citizens navigate the steep landscape with eighteen covered escalators and three moving walkways. The system runs downhill until 10 a.m., then uphill for the rest of the day.

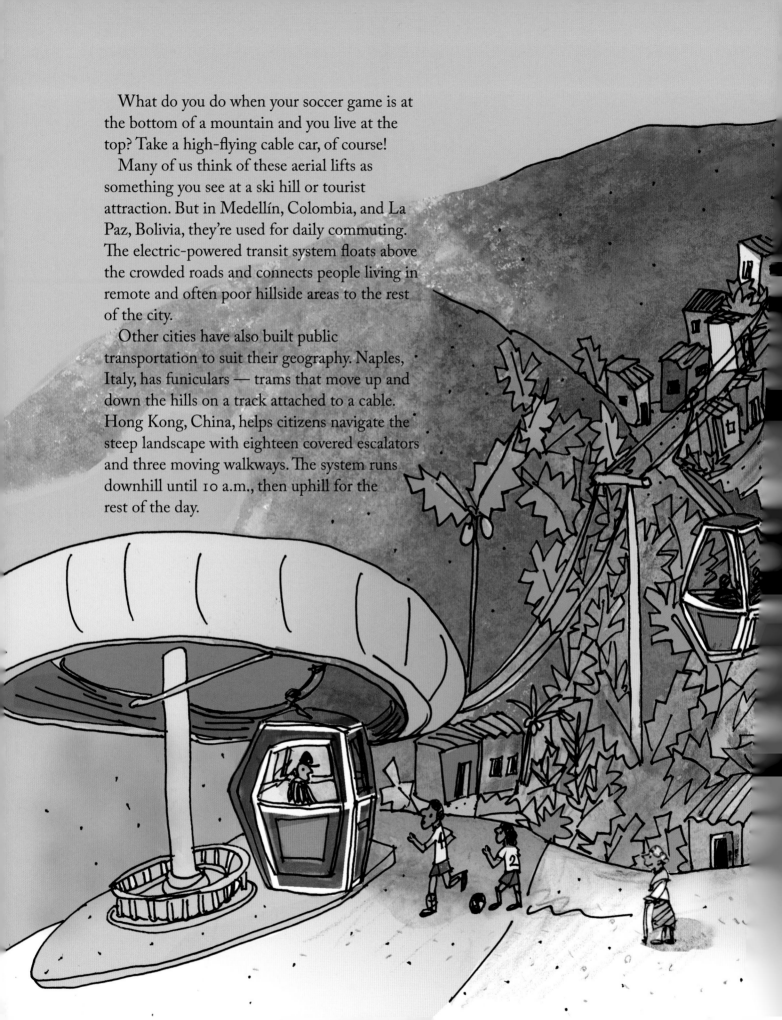

Did you know that many of the first cars ran on electricity? Gas-powered engines took over once mass production began, but now greener, cleaner electric cars are making a comeback. After 2030, many countries will ban the purchase of new gas vehicles.

To be truly green, the electricity should be sourced from renewable energy. The batteries used to store electricity are also important. They must be sustainably produced and recycled — with care for the environment and the workers who help make them.

Swapping one engine for another also doesn't solve the problem of endless traffic, or people stuck alone in their cars for long stretches of time.

But what happens if you take drivers out of the picture altogether?

Some people argue that self-driving electric vehicles will improve pollution and clogged streets since they will be used for carpooling, resulting in fewer cars and more space for transit and bike lanes. But lots of questions remain about safety, job losses for drivers and how self-driving vehicles will change our streets.

All over the globe, people ride bikes to school or just to buy an ice-cream cone, to haul packages, deliver food or get to work. There are cities in France and the Netherlands where children ride to school together on a pedal-powered bus! For some people with mobility issues, cycling can be easier than walking.

But for biking to be a true transit option, we have to slow traffic speeds and build streets that are geared to cyclists, including a network of safe, protected lanes across the city.

Many cities opened up new bike lanes during the pandemic. Paris, France, was already on its way to being a cycle-friendly superstar, with new lanes linking the city center to key suburbs. But during the crisis, the addition of pop-up bike lanes meant Parisians could cruise the city on more than 400 miles (640 km) of cycleways.

In Copenhagen, Denmark, traffic lights are coordinated so cyclists don't have to stop every block, making biking the quickest way to get around. All over the country, kids learn safe riding skills at specially built bicycle playgrounds.

Many cities also have bike-sharing schemes where you can borrow a bicycle for a small fee and return it to a docking station. These bikes are simple to use on the fly, just like a bus or streetcar.

Even the most committed city cyclists can be discouraged by bad weather, long distances or steep hills. But electric-powered bikes make getting around almost effortless. Using a combination of an electric battery and human-powered pedaling, they're one of the fastest-growing modes of city transit.

Most e-bikes are similar to regular ones but have a battery-powered boost. There are also e-bikes that look more like motorized scooters. Electric cargo bikes have big, comfortable compartments for passengers, which give kids a front-seat view of the street!

Electric skateboards and hoverboards are also popping up everywhere. And electric scooter–sharing programs, similar to car- or bike-share, have flooded cities such as Washington, D.C.

But these new electric vehicles are also raising big questions about speed limits, parking rules and how we can all share the road.

Pedestrians — including people who use wheelchairs and other mobility devices — are at the heart of city life. When we move at a slower pace we can stop to chat or smell a flower, maybe even notice ants building a city of their own!

Walkability is a measurement of how friendly a community is to pedestrians. Walkable cities are healthier and less polluted. They are accessible to everyone, whether eight or eighty years old, in a wheelchair or out for a run.

Walkable cities are also stronger economically because people love to live in these healthy places. Plus, the more we get out of our cars, the more we save on transportation and can spend money in local shops and markets.

So how do we build these cities?

We can start by dedicating space to pedestrians — wide sidewalks for playing hopscotch or setting up a lemonade stand. We can create signs and install lighting, as well as benches for resting in the shade of a big tree. We must plan and build neighborhoods where it's possible to live, work and shop for basic needs all in one area.

Slower road speeds, narrower streets and fewer cars make a city more enjoyable to explore on foot — and much safer. When Oslo, Norway, went almost entirely car-free in the city center in 2019, there were zero pedestrian and cycling deaths.

The hum of streets alive with people, music and conversation is part of the joy of cities. But amid all that racket and closeness we have to work hard to live and play well together.

How we move around — to school and work and everywhere in between — plays a big role in whether our cities run smoothly or are tangled in traffic and frustration. After all, the design of streets, sidewalks, bike lanes and transit hubs shapes every aspect of our lives.

Now more than ever, people all over the world are committed to building stronger, greener and more connected cities. Together we can push for walkable streets and transportation systems that put our health and the health of the planet first.

The time is now. Let's get moving!

What can we do to promote sustainable transportation?

• Start a green transportation or bike club at your school and host a Walk (or Bike) to School Day.
• Join other kids and parents to create a walking or cycling "school bus" and travel together. Agree on a route and pick up kids along the way.
• Ask your school to provide places to lock bikes and scooters.
   • Brainstorm ways to cut down on car trips that are less than a mile (1.6 km), and walk or bike instead. That will save money, reduce greenhouse gas emissions and pollution, and improve your health!
   • Could streets near your school be temporarily closed to motorized traffic at pickup and drop-off, like in Hackney, England?

- Are the crosswalks near your school or home safe? Seattle, Washington, has a program that supports neighborhoods to paint crosswalks in bright colors and designs to increase visibility.
- Ask your teacher to arrange transportation for your next class trip on the city bus, streetcar or subway.
- Write your city councillor to request more trees on your local streets. Trees slow down traffic and offer shade to pedestrians.
- Write and tell your mayor about cities such as Paris, France, and Toronto, Ontario, that offer free transit for kids under twelve. Ask your city to do the same!
- Could your city's public transit be better? Is it accessible to everyone? Does it serve all communities? Would it help if your city center went car free? Write to your local representatives to suggest how transit could be improved.

Glossary

Cable car: a vehicle that hangs from a continuously moving cable or is pulled along railway tracks by a cable.

Carbon dioxide: a colorless, odorless gas that is a mixture of carbon and oxygen (CO_2). People and animals breathe it out. Whenever something organic is burned, CO_2 is created. It is considered a "greenhouse gas," and it contributes to climate change.

Clean energy: energy such as electricity generated by solar or wind power that does not pollute the air and atmosphere when used.

Climate crisis / climate emergency: the serious problems caused or likely to be caused by changes in the earth's weather system — especially the world getting warmer as a result of human activities.

Diesel: a liquid fuel made mostly from crude oil and used in diesel engines.

Fossil fuel: coal, oil or natural gas formed from the remains of prehistoric plants and animals.

Funicular: a cable railroad on a mountain or hillside. Two cars — one going up, the other down — are attached to a single cable and counterbalance each other.

Magnetic levitation trains: very fast trains that use magnetic repulsion to move. The magnetic fields on the tracks and on the train itself repel each other so the train rises a small distance above the tracks. Floating on a cushion of air, there is no friction to slow it down. The same magnetic repulsion moves the train forward.

Mass production: the production of large numbers of a standard article (such as a car), often by assembly line or automation (as in a factory).

Omnibus: a horse-drawn public transportation vehicle dating to the early 1800s; the word was later shortened to "bus."

Public transportation: a system of vehicles such as buses, streetcars and trains that run on a fixed schedule for public travel.

Renewable energy: a source of power that is unlimited or can be restored, such as solar, wind, tidal, wave or hydroelectric energy.

Self-driving vehicle: transportation that is operated by technology that senses the environment around it and does not rely on a human driver.

Steam engine: an engine powered by steam that is created when coal or wood is burned in a boiler. The steam is forced into cylinders that push pistons, which drive the machine.

Sustainable: causing little or no damage to the environment, and as a result able to be continued for a long time.

Tram (sometimes known as trolley or streetcar): a transit vehicle that travels over rails and is usually connected to an overhead cable.

Transit: a system for carrying people or goods from one place to another on trains, buses and other vehicles (see also public transportation).

Transit hub: a place where passengers can switch between different modes of transit (as in a station where commuter trains stop and people can get on the city subway).

Selected Sources

Many sources were used to research this book. Students and teachers will find the following useful for further reading.

Gertsberg, Inna and Mike Lowery. *The Way Downtown: Adventures in Public Transit*. Kids Can Press, 2017.

Mulder, Michelle. *Pedal It! How Bicycles Are Changing the World*. Orca Book Publishers, 2013.

88ocities.org
bloomberg.com/citylab
schoolstreets.org.uk
treehugger.com/transportation/

These books offer insight and additional research possibilities for older readers.

Bruntlett, Melissa and Chris Bruntlett. *Curbing Traffic: The Human Case for Fewer Cars in Our Lives*. Island Press, 2021.

Grescoe, Taras. *Straphanger: Saving Our Cities and Ourselves from the Automobile*. HarperCollins Canada, 2012.

Newman, Peter and Jeffrey Kenworthy. *The End of Automobile Dependence: How Cities Are Moving Beyond Car-Based Planning*. Island Press, 2015.

Schiller, Preston L. and Jeffrey R. Kenworthy. *An Introduction to Sustainable Transportation: Policy, Planning and Implementation*, 2nd ed. Routledge, 2018.

Acknowledgments

Many thanks to Gil Penalosa, founder and chair of 8 80 Cities, as well as Laura Penalosa, Alejandra Penalosa and Camila Uriona, who provided invaluable insights into the possibilities of city living. I am also grateful to the entire Groundwood crew, who care deeply about making beautiful and meaningful books for children.